STOP JUST BEING YOURSELF!

Also by
J. Robb Cruser and Bill Mitchell

The Disruptive Lawyer's
Little Black Book of Litigation Management

The Disruptive Lawyer's
Little Black Book of Negotiation

Becoming Positively Disruptive

STOP JUST BEING YOURSELF!

Small Book/Big Change: A Shockingly
Simple System for Shattering Limits
and Living a More Abundant Life

J. Robb Cruser
Bill Mitchell

Although the author and publisher have made every effort to ensure that the information in this book was correct at the time of first publication, the author and publisher do not assume and hereby disclaim any liability to any party for any loss, damage, or disruption caused by errors or omissions, whether such errors or omissions result from negligence, accident, or any other cause.

Copyright © 2025 by J. Robb Cruser and Bill Mitchell

All rights reserved. No part of this book may be reproduced or transmitted in any form or by any means, electronic or mechanical, including photocopying, recording, or any information storage and retrieval system, without permission in writing from the author.

ISBN: 978-1-6653-1024-6

This ISBN is the property of BookLogix for the express purpose of sales and distribution of this title. The content of this book is the property of the copyright holder only. BookLogix does not hold any ownership of the content of this book and is not liable in any way for the materials contained within. The views and opinions expressed in this book are the property of the Author/Copyright holder, and do not necessarily reflect those of BookLogix.

Library of Congress Control Number: 2025908628

⊗This paper meets the requirements of ANSI/NISO Z39.48-1992 (Permanence of Paper)

061925

On Change

"Success is nothing more than a few simple disciplines, practiced every day."

—Jim Rohn

"What you are not changing, you are choosing."
—Laurie Buchanan

"Your life does not get better by chance, it gets better by change."

—Jim Rohn

"The measure of intelligence is the ability to change."
—Albert Einstein

On Excellence

"We are what we repeatedly do. Excellence, then, is not an act, but a habit."

—Aristotle

On Coaching

"Coaching is about helping people do more than they think they are capable of."

—John Whitmore

"The coach's job is not just to tell someone what to do, but to create an environment where they are encouraged to flourish and find their own solutions."

—Sue Enquist

"Meet them where they are; get them where they need to be."

—Anonymous

"A good coach can change a game. A great coach can change a life."

—John Wooden

Contents

Opening Challenge		ix
Introduction		xi
Chapter 1	Why Change?	1
Chapter 2	What to Change?	3
Chapter 3	How to Change?	7
Chapter 4	Life Change: An Example	15
Conclusion		19
Questions and Answers		23
Brutal Feedback		47
Acknowledgments		49

Opening Challenge

"Just be yourself."
—Unknown

"JUST BE YOURSELF." What if that's the worst advice you've ever been given?

I often see my happy-go-lucky retired neighbor and ask, "What's on the agenda for today?" With a playful grin, he always responds, "Well, I'm starting slow, then I plan to taper off." We both chuckle—it never gets old. If you're like my neighbor and basically satisfied with just being yourself—who you are and what you're doing—then congratulations. Few get to the self-satisfaction mountaintop. But this book isn't for you, because people who are satisfied with the rhythms of their lives typically don't change—they don't grow or adapt. Why should they? They're already satisfied. The status quo reigns.

This book is for those who, when told, "Just be yourself," respond, "Nope! I don't want to live a life of low expectations. I don't want to just be my current self—I want to expect better, do better, and be better." This book is for those who accept the challenge to not just be themselves, but to pursue a more abundant life in all their roles.

Introduction

"I can resist everything except temptation."
—Oscar Wilde

"I do not understand what I do. For what I want to do I do not do, but what I hate I do."
—Apostle Paul

The Change Struggle: Selfless Mind (Dr. Jekyll) v. Selfish Body (Mr. Hyde)

WHY IS ENDURING positive life change so darn difficult? Why can't we save more money? Eat healthier? Lose weight? Reduce stress/anxiety? Spend more time with family/friends? Volunteer more? Why do we so often act against our own best intentions—doing in the body, what we oppose in the mind.

STOP JUST BEING YOURSELF!

Because we all have a bit of Dr. Jekyll and Mr. Hyde[1] in us. Our better Dr. Jekyll side takes a selfless approach, seeking to care for others as well as ourselves. Meanwhile, our selfish, lazy Mr. Hyde side is already sprawled on the sofa, snack in hand, assuring us that 'just one more scroll' won't hurt — right after finishing the latest Netflix series, and caring only about himself. We'll never eliminate either; the mind/body duality inside us is real. This book's purpose is to facilitate positive life change that produces an abundant life by maximizing our Dr. Jekyll side while minimizing our Mr. Hyde side.

***

---

[1] Stevenson, Robert Louis. 1886. *Strange Case of Dr. Jekyll and Mr. Hyde*. London: Longmans, Green, and Co.

CRUSER MITCHELL

"Get off my lawn!"

—Walt Kowalski,
Clint Eastwood's character in *Gran Torino*

Anti-Hubris Pledge

We understand that any personal development book risks coming off as condescending, even hypocritical. After all, most readers have already achieved much—both personally and professionally—without the coaching of this or any other self-help offering. Perhaps it's wiser to stay on our own lawn (translation: mind our own business), focusing on the ample room for our own personal growth rather than meddling in the life change of others.

Point taken!

We don't have all the answers. Implement what makes sense; ignore what doesn't. Share your answers with us in the feedback section. Our goal isn't to preach; it's to share a system that has guided our own uneven, modest growth when we had the discipline to follow it rather than stray into hypocrisy.

***

CRUSER MITCHELL

"Resistance is futile!"

—The Borg, a fictional alien species in the Star Trek universe

Technology Addiction

Let's not pretend that technology doesn't already control us. The average American checks their phone 205 times per day and spends five hours daily using it,[2] second only to sleeping. Depressingly, that's 2.5 months per year looking at our phones. We are addicted to technology, our smartphones—for better, but mostly for worse. Resistance is futile.

Therefore, any system that promises to help organize our lives and achieve our goals without smartphones—the most dominant device in our daily lives—is fundamentally flawed. That's the

---

[2] Wheelwright, T. (January 1, 2025). Cell Phone Usage. https://www.reviews.org/mobile/cell-phone-addiction/.

reason we have a smartphone app at the center of our "system" to organize our lives and help us achieve our goals. If you can't beat them, join them.

***

"I have a system."

—Attributed to infamous fraudster Charles Ponzi

Our System

Stop Just Being Yourself: Small Book/Big Change: A Shockingly Simple System for Shattering Limits and Living a More Abundant Life, so says the title. A system? Give me a break! How many "sure-thing, get-rich-quick" schemes start with the claim "I have a system"? Buyer beware!

We make the opposite claim. Yes, we're sharing our life-change system, but realistically, the chance of quick success is zero. Lasting success is, at best, fifty-fifty—and that's being optimistic. In the pursuit of life change, many start strong, but few sustain lasting positive change. Consider the fate of most New Year's resolutions.

Okay, the "pep talk" is over.

What is the *goal* of our life-change system?

The goal is to move you closer to abundant living[3] in all your roles. An abundant life is one in which *you expand your positive impact on others by accomplishing more than you thought possible.* By expanding your positive impact on others, you're growing toward abundant living—the challenge of this book. An abundant life standard is illustrated by the fruit of the third tree.[4]

| What I'm Doing Now | What I Think I Can Do | Abundance | Full Potential |

---

[3] The abundant life standard versus maximizing full potential is more fully discussed in Question #1 of the Questions & Answers section.

[4] Illustration credit: Josie Cruser

What *is* our life-change system?

Our system is built on three foundational pillars: (1) adopting the right mindset, (2) simplifying goal setting, and (3) tracking goals/habits effectively—each working together to guide you toward abundant living in all your roles. Let's break them down.

Adopting the right mindset—means having an *overcoming, can-do* mindset, since setting significant goals is pointless without the belief that you can achieve them. Therefore, any impactful life-change system must adopt an overcoming, can-do mindset strong enough to defeat the three greatest self-limiting forces in the universe: the pull of the convenient status quo, the fear of failure, and the concern over what others think of us. How many goals have you failed to achieve—or never even attempted—for fear of failure, concern over what others may think, or a preference for the safety of the status quo? Harry Potter creator J.K. Rowling summed up this topic nicely: "It's impossible to live without failing at something unless you live so cautiously that you might as well not have lived at all. In which case, you fail by default." In today's social-media-driven culture, where approval is currency, the person who doesn't give a damn what others think is not only rare and powerful, but often happier—strong enough to reject the comfortable status quo and bold enough to chase something better. The right overcoming, can-do mindset is about being fearless, breaking from the herd, and moving closer to what once felt impossible—an abundant life.

Simplifying goal setting—means becoming positively *organized* by dividing your life into four manageable life *categories*: mind, body, spirit, and roles in life. Together, these categories define who you are. For each category, set a meaningful *goal*. And for each goal, build *habits* to achieve the goal. Too often, we live without margin, bouncing from one deadline to the next. Simplifying goal setting is about clarifying priorities, regaining control, and mostly getting organized.

Tracking goals/habits effectively—means becoming positively *accountable*, since setting significant goals is pointless without someone checking on your progress. Turning to *tools*, our system uses both a digital taskmaster—we chose the goal/habit tracking app called Strides[5]—and human ones: an enforcer and helpers. Effective goal tracking is all about accountability.

With our three-part life-transformation system in place, we now turn to the essential change questions: Why change? What to change? How to Change?

---

[5] There are many goal-setting/habit-tracking apps on the market. Pick one that works for you. Full disclosure: we have no financial or ownership interest in Strides – we're just a customer.

CHAPTER 1

Why Change?

"For of all sad words of tongue and pen,
The saddest are these: 'It might have been!'"
—John Greenleaf Whittier, *Maud Muller*

SUPPOSE I OFFER you ten million dollars. Do you take it?[6] But here's the catch. If you take the ten million dollars, you die tomorrow. Do you still take it? If you answered no, then you understand that the value of waking up tomorrow is worth more to you than ten million dollars.

---

[6] Full attribution to Minted Reality, https://www.tiktok.com/discover/minted-reality-if-i-offered-you-10-million-dollars

The lesson: Simply being alive is a precious gift that should not be squandered. Instead, we should strive to live abundantly in all our roles by being positively useful to others—to leave every situation better than we found it. So when our time comes, it will never be said of us, "What might have been."

CHAPTER 2

WHAT TO CHANGE?

*"There is nothing noble in being
superior to your fellow man; true nobility
is being superior to your former self."*
—Ernest Hemingway

TO LIVE ABUNDANTLY, we must be intentional about mindset and goal setting to avoid distraction and drift. What goals are important enough for you to define, organize, and commit to—pushing through the consistency and intensity challenges to achieve them? What would you have to accomplish to feel like you've met a goal or earned a personal or professional "win"? Without clearly defining what we want to change, it's difficult to reach unspoken goals.

Fortunately, our system helps answer this question: What to change?

The first pillar of our life change system starts with a simple directive: change your mindset. Reminder: to break free from the three greatest self-limiting forces—clinging to the stagnant status quo, fearing failure, and being overly concerned what others think of us—we must first believe that bold, positive change is possible. Without that belief, moving forward is futile, our efforts will likely fall short. That's why the first and most crucial step in change is clear: *choose* an overcoming, can-do mindset. Of course that's simple to say, but hard to do, but at some point there must be a mindset shift from being a victim of status quo to an agent of change. The choice is yours: embrace the stagnant status quo or adopt an overcoming, can-do mindset.

The second pillar of our life-change system—simplifying goal setting—helps get us organized.

This means structuring our goals around life's four fundamental *categories*: Mind, Body, Spirit, Roles in life. We start by ordering which categories matter most.[7] If you're a bodybuilder, "body" may be your top category. If you're an astrophysicist, "mind" may take precedence. Or if you're a minister, "spirit" probably comes first. You get the idea. For each category, establish a corresponding *goal*. And for each goal, create enough *habits* to achieve it. While everyone is different, here are some examples of what this organization process looks like.

---

[7] Important disclaimer: We do not seek to impose or endorse any particular viewpoint. If you don't prioritize the "spirit" or any other category, skip it, and focus on the categories that are important to you.

STOP JUST BEING YOURSELF!

Category	Accompanying Goal	Supporting Habit
Body	Lose 15 pounds in 6 mos.	-Limit ETOH to 3X per week. +2 mile walk with John 3X per week
Mind	Keep a sharp mind	+Solve daily Sudoku puzzle +Juggle for 30 seconds
Spirit	Grow in faith	+weekly church attendance
Role (i.e., father)	Maintain relationship w/ daughter at college	+write an encouraging text weekly +visit campus each semester

In summary, without the right mindset and a clear, organized approach to goal setting, meaningful life change is unlikely, leading back to the stagnant status quo. So, get your mindset right (pillar #1) and your categories/goals/habits organized (pillar #2) to have a genuine chance at moving closer to an abundant life—one that positively impacts many.

CHAPTER 3

How to Change?

*"Insanity is doing the same thing over
and over and expecting different results."*
—Albert Einstein

KNOWING WHY AND WHAT to change is the easy part—our rational Dr. Jekyll mind handles those with ease. But the *how*? That's a battle with our rebellious Mr. Hyde—our body, which cares little about mind-crafted goals. It's lazy, selfish, resists discipline, and defaults to doing nothing. How many good intentions lived in our minds but never made it into action because our body refused to follow? How do we do positive, goal-affirming actions when we don't feel like it—and resist negative, goal-stealing actions when tempted? Real change doesn't happen in the mind—it happens when the mind wrestles the body into motion. For true transformation, Dr. Jekyll must tame his wayward Mr. Hyde—day after day. But even the strongest minds can't win that fight alone. Dr. Jekyll needs help.

Enter the third pillar of our life-change system—effective goal/habit tracking powered by internal and external accountability—which is our key *enforcement mechanism* that brings the entire system to life. First, install a digital goal/habit tracker—like the Strides app—on your smartphone. It drives internal, self-directed accountability and keeps your goals top of mind.

Second, enlist people—trusted enforcers and helpers—for external accountability. They'll challenge us, support us, and help keep us on track. Together, this system of redundant accountability is the engine that turns good intentions into lasting positive change. Now, let's take a closer look at pillar three and its related tasks.

Task 1: Download a digital goal/habit tracker app to your smartphone.

Task 2: Consistent with your point of view, prioritize the key life categories—mind, body, spirit, and roles in life. For each selected category, input a clear goal, and enough supporting habits needed to achieve it. For conceptual clarity, list each entry using forward slashes: Category/Goal/Habit(s).

Task 3: Use the digital goal/habit tracker app to track your progress and keep you *internally* accountable as you pursue your life-changing goals.

Reality check. The truth is that a digital goal/habit tracking app alone is probably not enough to achieve our goals. Afterall, it still comes down to individual willpower to follow the app. Of course, we could be wrong. Perhaps some are like David "Stay Hard"

STOP JUST BEING YOURSELF!

Goggins[8] with big goals, super willpower, motivation, discipline, and a history of crushing goals. If that's you, keep up the great work! Don't worry about finding enforcers and helpers. Change nothing!

But for most of us, internal willpower isn't enough. Our lazy Mr. Hyde side is too strong within us. We need *external* support—we need people—which brings us to Task 4.

Task 4: Recruit an enforcer and some helpers to track your progress and keep you *externally* accountable. First, find an *enforcer*, benevolent or otherwise, to keep you closer to your selfless Dr. Jekyll side and away from your lazy, selfish Mr. Hyde side. The question is, what type of enforcer/coach works best for you? Do you respond better to the "carrot" or "stick"?

For example, Jensen Huang, billionaire and cofounder of Nvidia, is hardcore. He starts each day

---

[8] Author of the bestselling book *Can't Hurt Me: Master Your Mind and Defy the Odds.*

by looking in the mirror and telling himself, "You suck," as self-humiliation to stay hungry to meet the next goal. He applies this coaching practice to his employees, believing that occasionally humiliating one wayward employee is a "small price to pay for group learning"[9] and he can "torture his people into greatness."[10] Metaphorically speaking, that is.

On the other hand, you may respond better to the more laid-back coaching style of John Wooden, the legendary UCLA basketball coach, who neither humiliated his players nor argued with referees. Instead, he did most of his coaching during practice and, come game time, let the players play.

To each their own. The key is to know yourself and what type of coaching you best respond to. But we all need the right enforcer/coach to increase our chances of success. So, find your enforcer/coach,

---

[9] We do not endorse this coaching style.
[10] Tae Kim, "The Hard Work of Tech Mastery," *Wall Street Journal*, December 16, 2024.

share with them your plan, and have them hold you accountable.

Second, find some helpers—people who encourage you to stay committed to your new habits. These can be family members, friends, coworkers, or teammates who not only offer support, but may even join you in practicing your new habits, helping you stay consistent and energized. Just as important, helpers celebrate your wins—an essential part of staying motivated on the path to positive change. But when motivation fades or you begin to slip, that's when your enforcer steps in. They provide external discipline to keep you accountable and make sure backsliding doesn't go unnoticed. Think of helpers as the "good cops" and enforcers as the "bad cops"—working together to get you to your goals.

Importantly, enforcers and helpers make our goal *public*. It's no longer our little secret; it's out there now. We've got other people involved, so there's no turning back. So, incorporate helpers into your plan by inviting a friend on your planned weekday walks or other habits. Better yet, join the local track club to surround yourself with others pursuing the same goals. The more external support attached to the plan—enforcers and helpers—the greater your chances of building new habits and making progress toward your goals. If your plan is lacking an enforcer and helpers, that's a red flag that it lacks the external accountability necessary to succeed.

Task 5: Refining and Updating Goals.

Over time, some goals are successfully achieved, while others fade away. Priorities shift. Goals evolve. Circumstances change. It's important to periodically re-evaluate our life-change system—its goals and supporting habits—to ensure they still align with our priorities or need to be replaced with new ones.

In summary, by doing these five tasks, we are more likely to move along the pathway to an abundant life—one that positively impacts many.

The Abundant Life Pathway

WEEKLY WINS → NEW HABIT FORMATION → GOAL ATTAINMENT → ABUNDANT LIFE

CHAPTER 4

LIFE CHANGE: AN EXAMPLE

"A good example is the best sermon."
—Benjamin Franklin

LET'S USE AN example to illustrate how our system works. With your free Strides app in hand, let's begin.

Step 1: Identify the life *category* to change—mind, body, spirit, or role. In this example, the life category is body.

Step 2: Identify the related *goal*. Here, the body goal is to lose fifteen pounds in six months.[11]

---

[11] Apologies. We have better, less superficial goals in mind for all of us, but since this goal is a popular New Year's resolution in the United States most years, we use it merely for illustrative purposes.

Step 3: Identify the *habits* to support the goal, both the positive habits to do and the negative habits to avoid. Here, the positive habit is to take three two-mile walks per week with a friend, John. The negative habit to avoid is to limit alcohol intake to three times per week. Here's how our two sample entries appear in the Strides app.

Progress	Trends	Calendar	Rankings
Average Progress: 83%			2/2 on track
Body/-15lbs/alcohol limits			1/3 this week
Body/-15/2 mile walk w/John			2/3 this week

That's it. You are on your way. But these two habit entries are just the starting point. You'll need to formulate as many habits as necessary to achieve your stated goal, then incorporate them into your chosen app.

As for enforcers and helpers (external accountability), in our example, you plan to walk with John (helper), which is a smart strategy as it will make the walk more enjoyable and reduce the temptation to skip. Noticeably missing is the enforcer/coach figure. This is a red flag and needs to be remedied to increase the likelihood of success for this weight loss goal.

Notice in our example, we don't initially ask the app to track our weight. Why? Because progress is slow and often barely noticeable at first. Focusing on the end goal too soon can lead to frustration and might even cause us to abandon our goal altogether. It's better to measure end-goal progress after some time, say the thirty-day mark, allowing the benefits of accumulating weekly wins to take hold.

When We Stumble

We will stumble. We won't break all our bad habits or achieve every goal. It happens.

However, we don't have to be perfect to succeed. Suppose we completed our weekly walks for six out of eight weeks. Such consistent weekly wins demonstrate that we've formed a new habit—walking—something we now do regularly, albeit imperfectly. Our habit-changing strategies are working. As James Clear writes in *Atomic Habits*, habit formation is like an election. Every action we take is a vote either in favor of or against building that habit. Sometimes, achieving the goal is simply about winning by a slim margin—51 to 49 percent. In other words, focus on goal progress, not perfection.

Pick Your Pain

Paraphrasing entrepreneur Jim Rhon, "We must all suffer from one of two pains: the pain of discipline or the pain of regret." The commitment to the former pain is the dividing line between meeting your stated goals and enjoying a more abundant life versus getting stuck and living a middling life.

Conclusion

REMIND US AGAIN: what's so wrong with "Just Being Yourself?"

Nothing—if you're satisfied with a comfortable, predictable, and static existence. Many people stay locked in their ever-shrinking comfort zones, never pushing beyond the familiar status quo, and they seem just fine. But if that were enough for you, why would you be reading this book?

The truth is most of us carry a lot of the selfish, lazy, growth-resistant Mr. Hyde inside us—urging us to take care of number one (ourselves), shy away from failure or controversy, and worry far too much about what others think. And since Mr. Hyde lives in all of us, "Just Being Yourself" isn't a growth strategy—it's a comfort strategy. Stay there too long, and the day will come when it's said of us, "What could have been." And that's no legacy to leave. But going from a middling life that positively impacts few to an abundant life that positively impacts many won't happen on its own—it requires change.

And change takes a system. We're not claiming this is *the* system – but our system built on the three pillars of (1) an overcoming, can-do mindset, (2) organizing your life goals into four categories, and (3) being accountable to achieve them – is more likely to succeed than the tired advice of "Just be yourself" or "Try harder." Boiled down, to be effective our system uses the tools of a simple app and a few trusted enforcers and friends. Use our system and tools to resist your inner Mr. Hyde. Use them to expect better. Do better (not necessarily more). Become better. Or don't—stay the same. The choice is yours. But if the safe, familiar life isn't enough—if you seek to pursue a more abundant life that positively impacts many—then there's one thing you must do:

Stop Just Being Yourself!

| What I'm Doing Now | What I Think I Can Do | Abundance | Full Potential |

QUESTIONS AND ANSWERS

"The important thing is not to stop questioning. Curiosity has its own reason for existing."

— Albert Einstein

Question 1: What's your life standard: Doing more versus done enough?

Chapter 1 sets out the reason for change: don't waste our lives—never let it be said, "What might have been." But here's the tension: how do we balance the ambition to keep doing more for others and stay on the field with the peace of knowing we've done enough and can finally call it a day.

Answer:

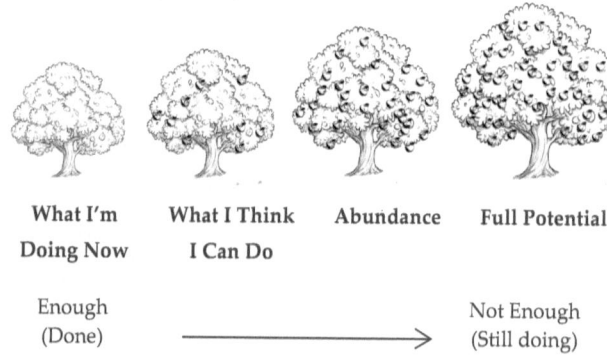

| What I'm Doing Now | What I Think I Can Do | Abundance | Full Potential |

Enough (Done) ⟶ Not Enough (Still doing)

This is one of life's great dilemmas—what standard we bring to living it. For some, there is no finish line and they never leave the playing arena. Take Albert Einstein—he was firmly on the not enough/still doing/ full potential side, working on his "unified field theory" on his deathbed, surrounded by his notes and handwritten equations. For others there is a finish line—the strivings cease. Take my "start slow and taper off" retired neighbor—he's on the enough/done side, content with what he's accomplished, and settling into the slow, quiet fade from the arena. And that's okay. Because at some point—whether by choice or by circumstance, we all cross that line. We all change from doing for others to others doing for us—it's the life cycle.

For those not ready to quietly fade away, this book advocates the abundance life standard—one in which you expand your positive impact on others by accomplishing more than you thought possible. It's the third tree with abundant fruit. Abundance is not about constantly maximizing the last drop of one's "full potential" in any given life category. We prefer the more achievable "abundant life" standard over "maximizing full potential," because the former suggests a sense of balance and sufficiency, while the later focuses on the unattainable, immeasurable ideal of one's "full potential."

To illustrate, say Diane Speedy sought to run a marathon in under three hours, believing that goal would "maximize her full potential." She spent countless hours training, dieting, and grinding through nagging injuries and fell short on her first attempt, clocking in at three hours and one minute.

On her second attempt, she succeeded, clocking in at two hours and fifty-nine minutes, achieving her goal. However, she didn't feel she had reached her "full potential," believing she could run even faster with more time and training. Perhaps her true "full potential" is an even faster time, say two hours and fifty-four minutes—who's to say? But would a five-minute improvement really add any meaning to her life, especially if it meant neglecting other important life categories—mind, spirit, and roles of life?

In summary, living an abundant life is like earning a B+ in any life category, while reaching full potential is comparable to achieving an A+. For Diane, a time of three hours and one minute represents abundance, while two hours and fifty-nine minutes symbolizes her full potential, at least until her next personal record moves the goalposts again. We endeavor to coach up people to elevate their lives from a C (Satisfactory), where many start, to B+/A– (Good approaching Excellent). For most, a B+ is good enough.

But expectations vary. Each person must choose which life categories to change and define their own standard of success in order to achieve their version of an abundant life. Metaphorically, the third tree symbolizes a life that bears abundant fruit. If that isn't enough, forge your own path and strive to become the maximizing "full potential" fourth tree with the most fruit. Go for it!

Question 2: How to Get the Right Overcoming, Can-Do Mindset?

Chapter 2 says that the first step in creating positive life change is to adopt an overcoming, can-do mindset. But isn't that easier said than done?

Answer:

Absolutely, mindset change is tough—but it's essential. Life will throw countless obstacles between us and our goals, so without an overcoming, can-do mindset, we'll struggle to keep moving when the inevitable challenges and hassles show up. Start with three simple steps (1) make the overcoming, can-do mindset *choice*, (2) set and achieve, small reinforcing actions, and (3) embrace realistic expectations. Together, these will help us build the right overcoming, can-do mindset essential for positive life change.

Returning to our weight loss example, first, regardless of what challenges and barriers arise, our response will be governed by an overcoming, can-so mindset to keep us going. Second, setting and achieving small habits—like taking the two-mile walk three times a week—reinforces that can-do, overcoming mindset. Finally, embrace realistic expectations, not to be confused with low expectations. Don't expect a straight path from setting your goals to achieving them. There will be setbacks, backslides, and occasional failures. And yes, the world is full of haters and doubters—expect them too. Nothing worth achieving comes easy. So don't let self-doubt or the noise of the negativity hustlers pull you into a self-limiting mindset that keeps you stuck in the status quo.

Question 3: What is a well-constructed goal?

Chapter 2 says, "To live an abundant life, we must be intentional about setting goals to avoid distraction and drift." But what is a well-constructed goal?

Answer:

In our weight-loss example, we started with the category "body." From there, we set the related goal: a fifteen-pound weight loss within six months. This is a well-constructed goal because it includes four key elements: it's written down, specific, realistic, and has a clear deadline.

First, it's written down, turning an abstract, invisible idea into a tangible, visible target. Second, it's specific, down to the very pound. Third, it's realistic and within our control. For example, wanting to be a professional basketball player like LeBron James or Caitlin Clark isn't realistic; that ship has sailed. Weight loss is completely up to us. Fourth, a deadline is crucial in goal setting. As the saying goes, "A goal without a deadline is just a dream."

One final thought on goal setting. A lot of people boss others around, thinking they know better. A lot of people think they know what goals others should pursue. And yes, some goals are statistically unlikely to happen—being a professional actor or athlete comes to mind. But each person must follow their own path and take their own chances, fully aware of the potential outcomes. So, make sure to pursue *your* goals, not those that you think others are pushing on you. If you're going to fail, fail while pursuing your own goals, not the goals of others.

Question 4: What is a well-constructed habit and how many should be included in a life change plan?

Answer:

A well-constructed habit supports the stated goal for any given category. New habits are intended to replace existing bad ones that keep us from our goal. In our weight-loss example, we listed two new habits: (1) three two-mile walks per week and (2) limiting alcohol to three times per week. If those two habits are enough to meet the stated goal—lose fifteen pounds in six months—then no more habits are needed. But what if they're not? Then what?

The basic idea is to identify the *enemies* standing between you and your goal and then craft habits—positive acts to do, negative acts to avoid—to defeat them. For weight loss, common enemies are (1) bad diet and (2) poor exercise. So, to improve our diet, we can add a habit to limit our daily mocha latte coffees to only twice a week. On the exercise side, we can add a habit to take the stairs at work or park farther from the entrance to get in some extra steps. Be creative in creating habits to defeat enemies standing in the way of your goals.

Question 5: You mentioned "roles in life" as a life category, could you expound on this concept?

Answer:

We each have different roles in life, such as son, daughter, sibling, spouse, parent, coworker, friend, provider, and so on—and we seek abundance in the relationships tied to these roles. But good relationships don't just happen, they must be nurtured. Going back to our father with a daughter going off to college out of state example, and his fears of losing touch with her. His system might look like this:

Life Category: Role (Father)

Goal: To maintain regular communication with his faraway daughter.

Habits: (1) Visit her at college once a semester for a weekend visit; (2) text her weekly with encouragement; and (3) send a handwritten letter to her twice a month.

Without a plan and system, we risk neglecting the relationships that give these roles meaning. Abundance means nurturing them with care, so they thrive instead of fading.

Question 6: What is the "spirit" life category about? Is this a religious book?

In chapter 2, you propose to structure goals around four fundamental life categories: mind, body, spirit, and roles in life. Then you add a disclaimer concerning the "spirit" category, saying, "[w]e do not seek to impose or endorse any singular viewpoint. If you don't prioritize the 'spirit' or any other category, skip it and focus on the categories that are important to you." Is that disclaimer really necessary?

Answer:

Yes. We want to be very clear that this is not a religious book; it's completely neutral. We do not seek to change anyone's point of view—political, religious, gender, sexual orientation, or otherwise. If you're a religious person, fine, use the spirit category. If you're not a religious person, fine, don't use the spirit category. It's none of our business what life categories you choose or prioritize. The limited purpose of this book is to share our app-plus-enforcers/friends system, helping you organize and advance your life categories and related goals—as you choose them—so you can move closer to living an abundant life, as you define it.

Question 7: Why is it important to use a goal/habit-tracker app? Won't a paper diary with a little discipline be enough?

Answer:

Okay, boomer. Strides—or whatever app or platform you choose—is an important tool because it eliminates a lot of our old excuses, like "Oh, I can't get organized" or "Oh, I can't regularly track my performance." Technology eliminates these old friction points. First, it provides an easy-to-use tool to *organize* our life-changing goals and habits. Second, it's mobile—the app lives on our phone—offering a daily *reminder* of our goals. Third, it *tracks* our weekly wins, motivating us to stay on track. Finally, it allows us to *visualize* our progress, complete with nifty charts and diagrams, building momentum during successes and redirecting our focus when we backslide. Let's see your paper diary do all that. For true life change to happen, sometimes the old dog must learn new tricks.

Question 8: The Consistency and Intensity Challenge

Chapter 2 challenges readers to identify goals that are important enough that they are willing to "push through the consistency and intensity challenges" to achieve them. What's the difference between consistency and intensity in the context of goal achievement?

Answer:

Some goals, like our weight-loss example, require long-term consistent effort. Others call for short-term intensity, and many require a blend of both. To be effective, your goal setting should strike the right balance between ambition and realism. Business coach Robin Sharma devised the "90/90/1" rule—dedicate the first 90 minutes of your day for the next 90 days to 1 big goal, without distractions or interruptions. For example, if your big goal is to prepare a one-hour marketing presentation within thirty days, ask yourself, Am I willing to spend 90 minutes for the next 90 days (i.e., consistency and intensity) needed to reach that one big goal? If you're ready to tackle the dual challenges of consistency and intensity to achieve the goal, go ahead and chase it.

Question 9: Behaviors vs. Habits

Chapter 4 says, "Identify habits to support the goal," using the example, "Take three two-mile walks per week with a friend, John," to support the weight-loss goal. Isn't it more accurate to say the proposed two-mile walk is merely a behavior or act that may (or may not) become a habit depending on if there's consistent follow-through?

Answer:

We're optimists. But you are correct. A habit is a "behavior that is *performed regularly*, and in some cases automatically."[12] If the two-mile walks don't

---

[12] Paraphrased from *Atomic Habits*, by James Clear, p. 6 (emphasis added).

happen regularly, then habit is the wrong term. They are mere wishful thinking.

Question 10:

In chapter 4, you used two example entries—limiting alcohol and increasing weekly walks—to demonstrate how to use the Strides app to set categories, goals, and habits. What are some other strategies to consider for accomplishing life changes?

Answer:

Other strategies to generally consider when formulating goal-supporting habits could include:

- Calendaring: Calendar the time and place of habit performance. For example, if you calendar the time, date, and place of your weekly two-mile walks, you'll be less likely to skip them.

- Nudges: Tomorrow's Prep Today

    Example: Setting out your walking clothes the night before to nudge you to remember to take your next day walk. Or having Strides send an audible reminder to take a walk.

- Friction: Establish barriers to avoid bad habits and reduce barriers to encourage good habits.

    Example: Deleting the Starbucks app, making it more difficult to indulge impulsively.

Question 11: Do habits create your identity, or does your identity create your habits?

Answer:

On page 32 of his bestseller *Atomic Habits*, James Clear presents this smoking example. He asks readers to imagine the responses of two smokers trying to quit when offered a cigarette. The first declines, saying, "No thanks, I'm trying to quit." The second also declines, saying, "No thanks, I'm not a smoker." Clear argues that the second response reflects a "shift in identity," as he no longer identifies as a smoker. The argument continues that such a shift in self-perception can drive lasting behavior change, making it more likely that the second person will consistently turn down the cigarette.

Are you persuaded? Can seeing yourself differently play a small role in a larger habit-changing plan? Maybe so. Adding to your Strides notes that you identify as a "regular exerciser" can help strengthen commitment in the context of our weight-loss example, especially when trying to avoid bad behaviors. But generally, we are more persuaded by Aristotle's teaching, "We are what we repeatedly do." Put simply, *over time*, our identity is determined by what we do—not by what we intend to do or claim to be. Only time will tell. If we end up never smoking again, our identity is that of a nonsmoker. If we relapse into smoking, our identity is that of a smoker. As the saying goes, "The road to hell is paved with good intentions."

Question 12: The Systems over Goals Conversation

In the context of life change, what's more important: stated goals or systems to accomplish stated goals?

Answer:

In his bestselling book *The Seven Habits of Highly Effective People*, author Stephen Covey emphasizes the need to "Begin with the End in Mind" (Habit 2), as goal setting provides the necessary focus to ensure our actions align with our desired outcome.

On the other hand, in the bestseller *Atomic Habits*, James Clear, channeling Dilbert cartoon creator Scott Adams, argues, "Forget about goals, focus on systems instead," explaining goals "are the results you want to achieve" while systems "are about the processes that lead to those results."[13]

---

[13] Scott Adams, *How to Fail at Almost Everything and Still Win Big: Kind of the Story of My Life* (Portfolio, 2013).

Forget about goals? That's unrealistic. Without a goal, nothing begins. But without a system, goals don't get done. So, generally speaking, we agree the emphasis should be on systems, but it never hurts to keep our "eyes on the prize" as well.

Question 13: The Success Sequence

What are three key decisions young people can make that are most likely to lead to an abundant life, one that positively impacts many?

Answer:

Sociologist Wendy Wang, Ph.D., defines the "success sequence" for young people as a three-step path to stability and upward mobility: (1) earning at least a high school diploma, (2) working full-time, and (3) getting married before having children—in that specific order, no deviation[14]. According to Dr. Wang's research, along with that of others, those

---

[14] https://www.wsj.com/articles/the-sequence-is-the-secret-to-success-1522189894

that followed all three steps had a poverty rate of "only 6 percent compared with 35 percent for their peers who missed one or more steps." Good to know, but did we really need a group of researchers to tell us what our parents, grandparents, teachers, and coaches have been preaching for years?

Question 14: Does pursuing a more abundant life—meaning, expanding your positive impact on others by accomplishing more than you thought possible—bring personal contentment?

Answer:

It sure helps. After achieving a semblance of independence and stability, most people pursue a combination of goals—some self-serving, and some aimed at serving others. For example, our weight loss goal is a personal, self-serving goal—there's nothing wrong with that. However, focusing too much on oneself creates a small world, a world of one. Sustained contentment usually comes from being *useful to others* within our communities. The more we contribute to others, the greater our sense of accomplishment and, ultimately, contentment. Finally, having high expectations for ourselves but lower expectations for others, also helps the personal contentment equation by reducing frustration brought on by the actions or inactions of others. But who can say for sure? Some people choose negativity despite their abundance and usefulness, while others choose positivity despite their poverty and limitations. People are curious creatures.

Question 15: How do I know if I'm living a more abundant life?
Answer:

Initially, you'll know by whether you're meeting your stated goals. But here's another simple daily test: when you meet someone new, skip the usual, "So, what do you do?"—which centers on the self—and instead ask, "So, what do you do . . . for the community?" This shift in perspective focuses on others. If you can easily answer that question yourself, it's a good indicator that you're living a more abundant, outward-focused life.

BRUTAL FEEDBACK

"You can't handle the truth!"

—Colonel Nathan Jessep, Jack Nicholson's character in *A Few Good Men*

IN OUR ANTI-Hubris Pledge at the beginning of this book, we admitted, "[w]e don't have all the answers. Implement what makes sense; ignore what doesn't. Share your answers with us in the feedback section."

And we meant it. We know this content can be greatly improved. Help us make it better, or at least, less bad. We can handle the truth (mostly).

Please share any feedback—the good, bad, or ugly—to feedback@stopjustbeingyourself.com.

Acknowledgments

THANK YOU TO Kathleen Kraynick for her key insight to focus on using a digital device as the key tool to enforce our "system" to achieve positive life change.

About the Authors

J. ROBB CRUSER and Bill Mitchell co-founded Cruser, Mitchell, Novitz, Sanchez, Gaston, Zimet, LLP—a law firm that has grown from one office with four attorneys into a nationwide practice with over one hundred lawyers across eight states.

www.cmlawfirm.com

www.ingramcontent.com/pod-product-compliance
Lightning Source LLC
Chambersburg PA
CBHW030535080526
44585CB00014B/946